PROVOKING THOUGHTS

101 Inspirational Quotes for Daily Life

Volume 1

NATASHA A. PIERRE

PUBLISHED BY: The Model Within, LLC.

ISBN-13: 978-1977706737
ISBN-10: 1977706738

PRINTED IN THE UNITED STATES OF AMERICA

INSPIRE ANOTHER!

SHARE THIS BOOK

Retail $15.00

Special Quantity Discounts

5-20 Books	$14.00
21-99 Books	$12.00
100-499 Books	$10.00
500+ books	$8.00

To Place an Order, Please Contact:

Sales: (813) 217-2893

Natasha@TheModelWithin.com

www.NatashaPierre.com

www.TheModelWithin.com

NATASHA A. PIERRE

The Ideal Speaker for your Next Event!

Personal Development Speaking Topics:

How to Ignite Your Passion & Discover Your Purpose
Transitions: How to Navigate Your Seasons of Change
How to Align Your Vision and Sight
Early Morning Success Habits

Professional Development Speaking Topics:

How to Find and Get Hired in a Career You Love
Overcoming Age as a Perceived Disability
How to Be Attractive in Business
Publicity Strategies that Win
Branding for Impact
And more!

To Book Natasha as Your Speaker:

Bookings: (813) 217-2893
Natasha@TheModelWithin.com
www.NatashaPierre.com
www.TheModelWithin.com

DEDICATION

I am fortunate to have some of the best people on the planet in my corner, encouraging me and reminding me that my words and inspiration would greater serve the world if they were in print and not only living on my computer. I share this accomplishment with you.

Many thanks to my immediate family:
Hollister, Sr. and Verdine, David & Nicole Hernandez,
Tsi-Ann, Ricardo and Marianne, Stacey & Randy Costin,
Kenya and Keisha, Kassandra, Hollister, Jr.
I am because you are. I did it!

To my Uncle Franky: You are my favorite!
Thank you for always checking on me.

To my inner circle of Catherine Cooper,
M. Janick Ferrier Hickman,
Nicole Ferri, Amber Shannon,
Kobie "Ocean" Dixon, P.P., LaToya James,
Hyacinth Tucker, Shinuh Holt -
Thank you for being in my corner,
for supporting my every endeavor,
and for being an available listening ear.
I love you for life.

To Lamman Rucker, Emme Vickers,
Kevin and Kelvin Curry, Theresa Royal Brown,
Rob and Cheryl Adams, Teddy Holloway -
Your friendship means the world to me.

Posthumously: Mr. Beauvais, I did it!

ACKNOWLEDGMENTS

"Inspiration is the thread in the fabric of my being."
-Natasha A. Pierre

Long before "inspiration" and "self-help" were
categories in bookstores and genres on which to
build a profession, I sought to be inspired.
As a child, I remember being disinterested in the
fictional required reading for school. In my private time,
I feasted on my parents' books written by authors like
Les Brown, Ben Carson and Warren W. Wiersbe.
It was something about their true stories,
words of encouragement and practical strategy
that drew me in, and made me feel alive!
My spirit was awakened with each chapter,
each paragraph and each line.

These inspirational books became journals as I highlighted,
underlined and wrote notes in the margins.
It was not *just* reading to me.
It was an opportunity for me to think, to plan
and to hope. It was an enjoyable experience with wonderful
accompanying feelings, and the more I read, the more
I knew that I wanted to recreate in others the same
wonderful feelings that these books created in me.

Inspiration is not just something I enjoy reading.
Inspiration is not merely what I want to give to the world.
Inspiration is who I AM, and who I have always been.

To My Mentors Senator Allison "Allie" Petrus, Rozell Burroughs, Berny Dohrman:
Thank you for seeing in me what I could not yet see in myself, and for caring enough to pour into me expecting nothing in return.

To Steve Cannonier, Ken Brewster:
Thank you for never allowing me to forget that I needed to share my gifts with the world.

To My Life Group Ladies:
It was your acceptance, love and support that ushered in the peace necessary to birth this project.

To Pastor Adelle Penn-Brown:
Thank you for demonstrating boundless living; for courageously standing in a category of one when it was not popular.

To First Lady Michelle Obama, Oprah Winfrey and Iyanla Vanzant: You are my sheros! Thank you for allowing your life to be my example.

To Johnathan M. Medlock:
You challenged me with this project,
and kept me accountable.
You are exactly who I need at this phase of my life.
Know that your presence is invaluable. I love you.

Natasha A. Pierre
Tampa, FL
October 31, 2017

FOREWORD

"I am very particular when I write a foreword because many people will read the foreward and use it to determine whether or not to purchase the book or to reshelve.

Natasha A. Pierre is a bold author, a Lady Leader, a phenomenal public speaker, a mentor, my long-time mentee and family to CEOSpace and to me personally.

For more than a decade I have endorsed Natasha's work to corporate clients, and have sent customer referrals to her that are respected industry leaders.
She is without a doubt the best of the best.

The book you hold in your hands, is a reset for your brain software. **Provoking Thoughts** is exactly what you need to level up your goal attainment and to defeat self-sabotage. Like taking a multivitamin, **Provoking Thoughts** is for your daily life. Natasha has created a 21st century bible to stay grounded and centered on purposeful priority living.

Natasha and I are both aware of how important it is to do the work necessary to keep the "computer above our necks" virus-free and loaded with smart programing. A daily reset means the difference between being the dreamer buried in the cemetery and you, the Super Achiever who risks everything to live on purpose, to secure their dreams and to make the dreams a reality for all of us to enjoy.

Provoking Thoughts carries my highest READ WITH CAUTION because you will quickly become addicted to the change in your thoughts and your productivity.

Reading **Provoking Thoughts** will lead to notes in the margin, making to do lists, meditation prompts, journal topics, decisions to make, action to take and paths to avoid. This book is virtually an up ramp to success for you, the reader.

As Chairman and founder of CEOSpace, the largest entrepreneur and professional institution serving 140 nations, for more than 30 years, and as the leading advocacy in Washington, DC for small business legislation, this is my special message to you:

Purchase **Provoking Thoughts** and then purchase ten copies of this book and give them to your family and friends.

Finally, I ask you to join me in sharing how this book has impacted your life. If you are touched like my family has been, then please take time as I have to share in elevating this work to the world.

I wish you all the effortless abundance that **Provoking Thoughts** will usher into your life. I so approve of this message."

Berny Dohrmann, Chairman
CEO SPACE INTERNATIONAL
Best Selling Author | Feature Film Producer

The Answer is "Yes"!

Yes!
Feel free to use any of my quotes in
your printed materials, on your websites
and on your social media, etc.

My **only request** is that you provide
me with appropriate credit by
printing my name along with the quote.

Thank you!
Natasha

HOW TO USE THIS BOOK

What is inspiration?

Inspiration is an influence that spurs us to action. It is an inner north star that guides us to that which truly satisfies us emotionally, mentally, physically, and every other "ly". Inspiration is a magnet. It attracts and draws to its existence everything necessary to establish and to maximize itself permanently. Inspiration seeks to live. It does not operate in a silo. It spreads, effects and transforms everyone and everything in its path. I believe inspiration is the light that Marianne Williamson spoke about in her quote *"as you let your light shine, you give others freedom to do the same."*

Inspiration is not religion-based. It can flow from religion, but stands independent of any label or confine because it is universal. It is for all. It is in all, and that is why we all seek it.

At the date of this printing, a Google search for "I need inspiration" yields 289,000,000 results in under 0.5 seconds. So, if you seek inspiration, know that you are not alone. Everyone seeks inspiration.

What separates us from animals is the unique awareness of inspiration as a necessary fuel for fulfillment in our daily activities. Without inspiration we are merely humans in search of inspiration.

Step 1: Write

This book is a collection of what I call divine downloads. When I received them, I wrote them down. Hence, I have already completed the first step for you.

Step 2: Meditate

Envisioning how a quote can impact your life will aid the transition into full implementation.
I recommend incorporating each quote that resonates with you into your daily meditation practice.

Step 3: Journal

For many people, it usually takes time to adopt new patterns of thinking and behavior.
If meditation aligns your thoughts, then journaling will align your behavior. Use the quotes as prompts for your daily writing and create a space for you to safely question all areas of your life. Be kind to yourself as opposition surfaces. The opposition is coming up to go out.

Step 4: Own It

Writing, meditating and journaling are only half of the process. Moment by moment, day by day, as you endeavor to incorporate these quotes into your life, they will take root. However, you must be willing to do the work.

Step 5: Share

I am sharing these quotes with you for you to share them with your circle. Let us all get wiser together. You have my permission to share these quotes. All I ask is that you provide me with appropriate credit by printing my name along with the quote.

1

When you commit
to your dream,
you become the
cause, not the
effect of your life.

2

Closure

may not come.

Resolve to

Move on <u>anyway</u>.

3

Fatigue is your enemy.

Go to Bed.

Get Some Rest.

4

Maturity is

owning your role

in a disappointment.

Owning is a
prerequisite
for progression.

5

You have **permission**
to change your mind,
and to change it again
and again and again.

6

Love yourself enough to be **unmoved** by how many people are upset by your choices.

7

Devoid of another's <u>interpretation</u> of who/what God is, you are free to truly explore your **I AM.**

8

Everything

cannot be spoken

in a whisper.

Sometimes you

must **SCREAM**

to be heard!

9

Mistakes do not disqualify you from future success. They **establish** your future eligibility.

10

Easy is the decision that is **not** yours to make.

11

Knowledge

is <u>not</u> power,

it is responsibility.

To **know** is

to be responsible.

12

If your yesterday
is more attractive
than your today,
play time is over.
It is time to
get to work.

13

Never beg
for anything you
can **freely** receive.

14

Someone who treats your today like your yesterday, does not deserve to be in your **tomorrow**.

15

The person that
is too <u>impatient</u>
to sit through
your sadness
is **disqualified** from
standing in your joy.

16

Ignoring your
gut feelings today
will lead to
headache and
heartache tomorrow.

17

Make peace
with being
misunderstood
and disliked.
It is a part of life.

18

Where you want to go
must speak louder
than where
you have **been**.

19

Never define
who you are
by what
you have **lost**.

20

Integrity starts with "I". Integrity must be a **personal** goal before you can demand it of others.

21

As you mature,

the goal is

not to care LESS,

but rather,

to care

DIFFERENTLY.

22

Some people
may **ONLY** desire
for you to be
the "Robin"
to their "Batman".

23

Your **PASSION** is the internal generator that kicks in when your power *(family and friends)* goes out.

24

The only currency you have is <u>NOW</u>.
Spend it wisely.

25

When you know how best looks, good is **unacceptable.**

26

When you

are growing,

EVERYTHING

is subject to change.

Do <u>not</u> get attached.

27

After age 21,
stop blaming your
parents and teachers.
Tag! You're it!

28

Passive aggressive behavior announces your immaturity. Have the **courageous conversations.**

29

Success does not manifest from doing <u>everything</u> perfectly, but rather from doing the right things **consistently**.

30

Is it that you "***can't***" or that you "***won't***"?

31

If you refuse
to learn the lesson,
you will
take the test again
and again and again
until you pass it.

32

The hardest part of honesty is **leading** up to telling the truth.

33

Maturity is choosing to embrace gratitude and to **reject** the dissatisfaction of the moment.

34

A lost battle

does not mean

a lost war.

35

Is it disability or personality?

36

Sometimes

you will receive

second chances.

Sometimes

you **will not**.

37

No matter
how much good
you want for someone,
it is still their **choice**
to choose otherwise.

38

There are some things that being beautiful (handsome) **cannot** fix.

39

A friend

sees your flaws,

and sticks around

anyway.

40

The person who
has lied to you
the most, is **you**.

41

Grow up willingly
or your immaturity
will **create**
opportunities
for you to do so.

42

Life is like
a power strip.
Sometimes you must
unplug from what
serves you **LEAST**
and plug in to
what will serve you
BEST.

43

You are
one **ROUTINE**
away from success.

44

Where there is **PASSION**, boredom dies. Boredom and passion cannot occupy the same space.

45

What you **DO** is greater than what you **PLAN**.

46

Mountaintop experiences are great, but some life lessons are **only** learned in the valley.

47

Struggle is relative.

Your story may

cripple one

yet be a **vacation**

to another.

48

An effort a day
keeps failure **away**.

Remember

who remembers.

Remember who forgets.

Notice

those who haste.

Notice those who delay.

50

Everyone
cannot <u>have</u> access
to your life.

Everyone
cannot **handle**
access to your life.

51

Be your **#1 Fan.**

52

Great family
and friends
make **counterfeits**
easy to identify.

53

Delayed

confrontation

will lead to conflict.

54

Sometimes the answer is "**no**" simply because you <u>cannot</u> yet handle the **responsibility** of "yes."

55

You are **not** better than anyone. You simply have different flaws.

56

What you truly believe will be evidenced in your **response** to a crisis.

57

Your family may be
the **last** to embrace
your evolution.
Evolve anyway.

58

People are telling you who they are.

Do not choose to **overlook** it.

59

People cannot

support you

beyond

their own fears.

60

To become a person
you admire,
you must *actually*
become a person
you admire.

61

Sometimes the greatest position of strength is in <u>allowing</u> someone to **BELIEVE** that they are stronger.

62

Stop telling your
valuable information
to people
who do not **value**
confidentiality.

63

Beauty must be
self-defined.

You can only
be tempted
by something
you **want**.

65

Define a person <u>not</u> by what they **HAVE**, but by what they **DID** to get it.

66

Prolonged
lack of knowledge
is a **self-inflicted**
wound.

67

Repeating a lie
over and over
will **not** make it true.

68

Live from
imagination,
not from memory.

Life is <u>equal</u> parts

see, say and do.

70

Sometimes when things do not add up, it is time to **subtract**.

71

Forgiveness
is for **YOU**,
not for
the other person.

72

Spending too much
time focusing
on what is **wrong**
leaves little time
to focus on
what is **right**.

73

Leadership begins **long before** your first follower arrives.

74

Your purpose is not to be the **carbon copy** of someone else.

75

A half truth

is still a **WHOLE** lie.

76

Walking in purpose
is **attractive**.

77

The goal is
to know **who** God is,
not to **find** God.

78

Function as if the answer is already "**YES**".

79

Gratitude creates
more opportunities
to be grateful.

80

Better to be chosen
than to be a choice.
Chosen is **definitive**.
Choice is **optional**.

81

"Everybody plays the fool, sometimes"

... but, please do not make foolish a **lifestyle** or your **residence**.

82

Compassion requires **action**, not merely **observation** and **opinion**.

83

The "**how**" emerges as you begin walking toward the "**why**".

84

You cannot expect people to love, support and be patient with the areas you **refuse** to confront and to correct.

85

You can have
an opinion and
operate in kindness
at the same time.

86

How do you know you have forgiven?

When you **stop** retelling the story.

87

Wealth is the **by-product** of a life lived with **passion** and with **purpose**.

88

"Loving others as yourself" can only work if you are **very good** at loving yourself.

89

Sometimes all you need to move forward is **not** the certainty that your way is **right**, but that the alternative is **definitely wrong**.

90

Sooner or later who you *"pretend to be"* and who you *"really are"* will meet. A **duel** will ensue.

Who will win?

91

You may not be able to determine **everything** that will happen, but you can choose your **response**.

92

Do not wait for all pieces of the puzzle to emerge. Start using the pieces you have **right now.**

93

Your focus
will determine
your **direction**
and **destination**.

94

The change you seek
is found in the
part of you that
you do **not**
want to change.

95

Sometimes
it is okay
to do good
for nothing
... in return.

96

Motivation

lasts for a <u>moment</u>.

Inspiration

lasts for a **lifetime**.

97

Sometimes you
outgrow people,
not because their life
is worth **LESS**,
but because your time
is worth **MORE**.

98

The most **important**
conversation
you will have today,
will be with **yourself**.

Life happens.
Okay, but how
will you **win**?

100

Do not become **addicted** to your story of hurt.

101

"When you can
no longer be held
captive by the fear
of revealed truth,
what remains
is **freedom absolute**."

MY FAVORITE QUOTES

1. We fall short because we do not know our purpose, we ignore it, or we live contrary to it. - Xaviera L Bell
2. Never discuss your problems with someone incapable of solving it. - Dr. Mike Murdock
3. I never learned hate at home, or shame. I had to go to school for that. - Dick Gregory
4. When they go low, we go high. - First Lady Michelle Obama
5. I hated every minute of training, but I said, 'Don't quit. Suffer now and live the rest of your life as a champion.' - Muhammad Ali
6. There is a special place in hell for women who do not help other women. - Madeleine Albright
7. I don't go by the rule book... I lead from the heart, not the head. - Princess Diana of Wales
8. Happiness doesn't result from what we get, but from what we give. - Ben Carson
9. Lots of people want to ride with you in the limo, but what you want is someone who will take the bus with you when the limo breaks down. - Oprah Winfrey
10. Life is not fear or unfair! Life is life, and you need to play the hand you're dealt. - James Malinchack

10. My spirit is too ancient to understand the separation of soul & gender. - Ntozake Shange

11. I'm a woman. Phenomenally. Phenomenal woman. That's me. - Maya Angelou

12. Love makes your soul crawl out from its hiding place. - Zora Neale Hurston

13. Imperfection is beauty, madness is genius and it's better to be absolutely ridiculous than absolutely boring. - Marilyn Monroe

14. One of the truest tests of integrity is its blunt refusal to be compromised. - Chinua Achebe

15. When life knocks you down, try to land on your back. Because if you can look up, you can get up. Let your reason get you back up. - Les Brown

16. Truth without love is brutality, and love without truth is hypocrisy. - Warren W. Wiersbe

17. You have to be reasonable with yourself and not feel guilty when things aren't perfect. - Jaclyn Smith

18. Call a thing a thing. - Iyanla Vanzant

19. The future rewards those who press on. I don't have time to feel sorry for myself. I don't have time to complain. I'm going to press on. - President Barack Obama

20. I want one momet in time when I'm more than I thought I could be. When all of my dreams are a heartbeat away and the answers are all up to me. - Whitney Houston

"What I learn, I teach.
What I receive, I share."
-Natasha A. Pierre

Thank you for allowing me to share
my life lessons with you!

ONE LAST MESSAGE

I'm so proud of you for making the great decision to enhance your life by reading the quotes in this book. I truly admire and respect you for wanting to invest in YOU!

My mission with this book was to serve you and to make a positive impact in your life by inspiring you to think and to act differently.

Even if only one quote inspired you to change a limiting belief or self-defeating behavior, then I am pleased.

Congratulations!

You did it!

ABOUT THE AUTHOR

Natasha A. Pierre is an award-winning speaker and Certified Professional Life Coach with over 20 years of experience in providing coaching, training and development to individuals, small businesses and corporations. She has successfully assisted audiences across the country with establishing clarity and creating the strategy necessary to boldly achieve their personal and professional life goals.

Her relatable style has allowed her to connect with global audiences to share her story of resilience, reinvention and living each day with purpose-consciousness.

> *"I've been blessed to do many things all because I followed my passions, and my passions led me to my purpose,"* states Natasha. *"It is my life's work to teach others how to do the same."*

Natasha's varied background also includes several successful business ventures, working as a professional model and actress with the Screen Actors Guild, as well as radio and TV broadcasting. In addition to her professional experience, Natasha graduated from Duquesne University with a B.A. in Mass Communications, and she has a Work Incentives Practitioner credential from Cornell University. Her additional certifications include: Supported Employment and Ministry.

Made in the USA
Columbia, SC
09 September 2021